W9-AOK-184

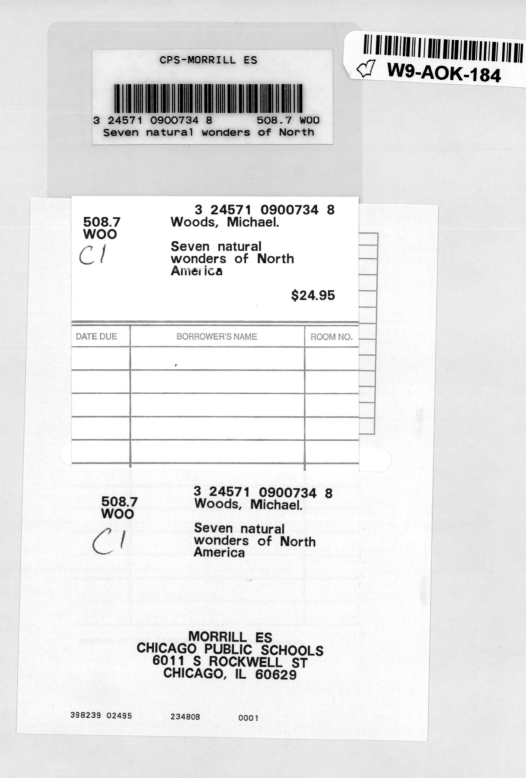

508.7
WOO

C1

3 24571 0900734 8
Woods, Michael.

Seven natural
wonders of North
America

$24.95

DATE DUE	BORROWER'S NAME	ROOM NO.

508.7
WOO

C1

3 24571 0900734 8
Woods, Michael.

Seven natural
wonders of North
America

7

Seven Natural Wonders of
NORTH AMERICA

Michael Woods and Mary B. Woods

TWENTY-FIRST CENTURY BOOKS
Minneapolis

To Natalie & Jerry Gavin

508.7
Woo
C1
$24.95
2011

Twenty-First Century Books
A division of Lerner Publishing Group, Inc.
241 First Avenue North
Minneapolis, MN 55401 U.S.A.

Website address: www.lernerbooks.com

Library of Congress Cataloging-in-Publication Data

Woods, Michael, 1946–
    Seven natural wonders of North America / by Michael Woods and Mary B. Woods.
        p. cm. — (Seven wonders)
    Includes bibliographical references and index.
    ISBN 978–0–8225–9069–9 (lib. bdg : alk. paper)
    1. National parks and reserves—North America—Juvenile literature. 2. Natural monuments—North America—Juvenile literature.
3. National parks and reserves—United States—Juvenile literature. 4. Natural monuments—United States—Juvenile literature. I. Woods,
Mary B. (Mary Boyle), 1946– II. Title.
E43.5W66 2009
917—dc22   2008021864

Manufactured in the United States of America
2 – DP – 4/1/10

Contents

Introduction —— 4

1 DINOSAUR PROVINCIAL PARK —— 7

2 PACIFIC RIM NATIONAL PARK —— 15

3 REDWOOD FORESTS —— 25

4 NIAGARA FALLS —— 33

5 THE GRAND CANYON —— 43

6 YELLOWSTONE NATIONAL PARK —— 53

7 PARICUTÍN VOLCANO —— 63

Timeline —— 70
Choose an Eighth Wonder —— 72
Glossary and Pronunciation Guide —— 73
Source Notes —— 74
Selected Bibliography —— 75
Further Reading and Websites —— 76
Index —— 78

INTRODUCTION

*P*EOPLE LOVE TO MAKE LISTS OF THE BIGGEST AND THE BEST. ALMOST 2,500 YEARS AGO, A GREEK WRITER NAMED HERODOTUS MADE A LIST OF THE MOST AWESOME THINGS EVER BUILT BY PEOPLE. THE LIST INCLUDED BUILDINGS, STATUES, AND OTHER OBJECTS THAT WERE LARGE, WONDROUS, AND IMPRESSIVE. LATER, OTHER WRITERS ADDED NEW ITEMS TO THE LIST. WRITERS EVENTUALLY AGREED ON A FINAL LIST. IT WAS CALLED THE SEVEN WONDERS OF THE ANCIENT WORLD.

The list became so famous that people began imitating it. They made other lists of wonders. They listed Seven Wonders of the Modern World and Seven Wonders of the Middle Ages. People even made lists of undersea wonders.

People also made lists of natural wonders. Natural wonders are extraordinary things created by nature, without help from people. Earth is full of natural wonders, so it has been hard for people to choose the absolute best. Over the years, different people have made different lists of the Seven Wonders of the Natural World.

This book explores seven natural wonders from the continent of North America. Like Earth as a whole, North America has far more than seven natural wonders. But even if people can never agree on which ones are the greatest, these seven choices are sure to amaze you.

A WONDERFUL CONTINENT

North America includes the nations of Canada, the United States, and Mexico. It also includes Greenland, a large island in the North Atlantic Ocean, as well as smaller Atlantic islands farther south. North America is the third largest of Earth's seven continents. Only Asia and Africa are larger. Almost 530 million people call North America home.

North America has a variety of fascinating natural features. They range from thick forests along the Pacific coast to rugged canyons in the southwestern United States to volcanoes in Mexico. North America also abounds with living wonders. Grizzly bears, wolves, coyotes, moose, and other big animals live in the Yellowstone River valley. Thousands of gray whales swim along the coast of Vancouver Island in the Pacific Northwest.

WONDERFUL ADVENTURE

This book will take you on a tour of some of North America's natural wonders. One stop on the tour will be Niagara Falls, the continent's most famous waterfall. The falls have long been a favorite spot for honeymooners as well as daredevils. Another stop will be the redwood forests of southern Oregon and northern California. These forests are home to the tallest trees on Earth. The tour will also visit a place where dinosaurs once roamed the land. In modern times, all that's left are the dinosaurs' bones. You will also visit a fantastic place with geysers, bubbling mud pools, steaming hot springs, and other amazing sites. Other fascinating places are waiting in between. Read on to begin your adventure.

Steaming hot water from the Old Faithful geyser in Yellowstone National Park rises 170 feet (50 meters) into the sky.

1 Dinosaur
PROVINCIAL PARK

*J*OSEPH B. TYRRELL, AN EXPLORER AND MAPMAKER, WAS WORKING ALONG THE RED DEER RIVER, NEAR DRUMHELLER, ALBERTA. ALBERTA IS A CANADIAN PROVINCE (A REGION SIMILAR TO A U.S. STATE). TYRRELL WAS PART OF A GOVERNMENT EXPEDITION TO EXPLORE WESTERN CANADA. EXPEDITION MEMBERS WERE LOOKING FOR COAL, OIL, AND OTHER NATURAL RESOURCES. THE YEAR WAS 1884. IN THOSE DAYS, WESTERN CANADA WAS A WILD LAND. FEW PEOPLE HAD EXPLORED THE REGION.

Near the banks of the river, Tyrrell noticed a strange object buried in the dirt. When he cleared away the dirt, he was amazed to discover that the object was a huge dinosaur skull. Expedition members loaded the skull into a horse-drawn wagon and took it to scientists in the nearby city of Calgary.

This skeleton of an Albertosaurus is on display in the Royal Tyrrell Museum in Drumheller, Alberta. Until Joseph Tyrrell found an Albertosaurus skull in 1884, scientists did not know about the dinosaur.

The scientists determined that the skull was from a previously unknown dinosaur. Scientists named the creature *Albertosaurus*, in honor of the province of Alberta. When scientists explored the area years later, they realized that Tyrrell had discovered a scientific treasure. The area around Drumheller had one of the world's richest deposits of dinosaur bones.

ANCIENT REPTILES

Joseph Tyrrell had discovered a gigantic dinosaur graveyard, filled with the skeletons of thousands of dinosaurs. The creatures had roamed western Canada in prehistoric times. Dinosaurs appeared on Earth around 225 million years ago. For almost 150 million years, they reigned as Earth's largest land animals. The largest dinosaurs weighed more than six elephants. Some were tall enough to look into a sixth-floor window. Dinosaurs became extinct around 65 million years ago.

Dinosaurs were prehistoric reptiles. Reptiles are animals that have dry, scaly skin and that breathe air into their lungs. Modern lizards, turtles, alligators, crocodiles, and snakes are all reptiles. Most reptiles live in warm, wet places.

Modern-day Alberta has very cold weather. Temperatures in winter can dip to −48°F (−44°C). The area is also dry, with only 16 inches (40 centimeters) of rainfall each year. Dinosaurs would have been unable to live in such a harsh climate.

But in prehistoric times, Alberta had very different weather. It was warm and wet year-round. The weather was ideal for dinosaurs. Dense forests covered parts of the land. Other places were open grasslands, where rivers flowed. The land had lots of plants and small animals for dinosaurs to eat.

DINOSAUR BONEYARD

Often, when an animal dies, its body rots quickly. Insects and other animals eat its flesh and bones. Within a short time, the body is completely gone.

Sometimes, however, the bodies of dead animals are preserved. For instance, if a dead animal is buried under a thick layer of soil, insects and other animals can't easily get to it. Its flesh will usually rot away underground. But the bones might remain intact.

In prehistoric times, Alberta's environment was perfect for preserving dinosaur bones. Its many rivers carried large amounts of sediment, a mixture of mud, sand, and minerals. The rivers often overflowed their banks and flooded the surrounding land. When the floodwaters pulled back, they left a thick layer of sediment on the land. That sediment could bury a dead dinosaur very quickly. Sometimes, rivers swept up the bodies of dead dinosaurs. The bodies floated downstream to sandbars. Eventually, layers of sediment covered the dead bodies. In these ways, sediment from Alberta's rivers created dinosaur graveyards.

WELCOME BACK

Over millions of years, more sediment covered the dinosaur bones. The muddy sediment slowly hardened. It eventually turned into layers of rock, such as sandstone, limestone, and shale. (These rocks are called sedimentary rocks, because they started out as sediment.) Dinosaur bones and whole skeletons were encased inside the layers of rock.

Millions of years later, rivers, rain, and wind wore away some of the rock that buried the bones. The dinosaur bones once again emerged above the ground. That's how Joseph Tyrrell found the skull of *Albertosaurus* along the Red Deer River in 1884.

The Red Deer River runs through this valley in Alberta. Over millions of years, sediment piled up, creating layers of rock. Rains, rivers, and floods eventually wore away the rock. This type of eroded landscape is known as badlands.

T. REX'S *Canadian Cousin*

Albertosaurus, the first dinosaur discovered in Alberta, lived about 70 million years ago. It was about 30 feet (9 meters) long and weighed about 4,000 pounds (1,814 kilograms). **Albertosaurus** ate other dinosaurs. It walked on two big hind legs. Dozens of large, sharp, banana-shaped teeth filled its huge jaws.

"The richest dinosaur fossil beds ever worked."
—Paleontologist Barnum Brown, describing the Red Deer River region, 1915

In the 1910s, American paleontologists (scientists who study the remains of prehistoric plants and animals) Barnum Brown and Charles Sternberg started digging along the river. Brown and Sternberg found thousands of dinosaur bones. The bones were preserved in good condition. Some were whole skeletons. Others were separate bones that had washed up into "bone beds." These piles contained hundreds of individual dinosaur bones.

AMAZING CREATURES

Since these early discoveries, paleontologists have found bones from almost forty different species, or kinds, of dinosaurs in southern Alberta. The discoveries include more than 150 complete dinosaur skeletons. Some of the dinosaur species were unknown until their bones were found in Alberta.

One species was *Styracosaurus*. Its name means "spiked lizard." This dinosaur was 18 feet (6 m) long and 6 feet (2 m) tall and weighed 6,000 pounds (2,720 kg). It had sharp horns on its face and head. A big horn on its nose measured 2 feet (0.5 m) long and 6 inches (15 cm) thick. Any enemy that tried to bite *Styracosaurus* on the face would have been very sorry.

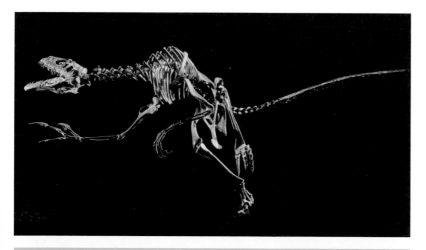

This dinosaur skeleton, one of more than one hundred found in the area of Dinosaur Provincial Park, looks ready to attack! This Dromaeosaurus, or "running lizard" in Greek, was a small, vicious hunter about 6 feet (1.8 m) in length and weighing 33 pounds (15 kg).

Another Alberta dinosaur was *Edmontonia* (named for Edmonton, the capital of Alberta). This dinosaur was built like an army tank, with thick scaly plates all over its body. They protected *Edmontonia* from the sharp spikes of enemy dinosaurs. *Edmontonia* was 23 feet (7 m) long and 6 feet (1.8 m) tall. It weighed 8,000 pounds (3,629 kg)—as much as an elephant.

> *"[Dinosaur Provincial Park] is arguably the richest dinosaur site in the world."*
> —Philip Currie, Royal Tyrrell Museum, 1997

PRESERVING THE WONDER

For years anyone could go into the dinosaur graveyard and collect bones. People sometimes took away the bones they discovered, so scientists couldn't study them. In 1955 the Canadian government decided to protect the bones. It created Dinosaur Provincial Park. The park covers 28 square miles (73 square kilometers).

According to park rules, scientists can still dig up dinosaur bones in the park. But they must get a government permit first. Park visitors who are not scientists cannot dig for bones or walk through certain areas of the park. These rules keep tourists from accidentally stepping on and damaging bones.

Paleontologist Phil Currie (far left) and his team excavate rock near Dinosaur Provincial Park in hopes of discovering more prehistoric remains. Digging within the park's limits is restricted.

A lifelike statue of an Albertosaurus greets visitors to the Royal Tyrrell Museum in Drumheller. It is one of the best paleontology museums in the world.

THAT'S A *Mouthful!*

Visitors to the Drumheller Visitor Information Center in Alberta can see "the world's largest dinosaur." This attraction is not a real dinosaur skeleton, however. Instead, it is a statue made from steel and plastic. It looks like a *Tyrannosaurus rex*, but it's about four times larger. It measures 86 feet (26 m) tall and 151 feet (46 m) long and weighs 145,000 pounds (66,000 kg). Visitors can climb up through the dinosaur's body to its mouth. The mouth is so big that twelve people can stand inside it at once. Looking out through the dinosaur's giant teeth, visitors can admire the scenery around Drumheller.

Visitors can take tours of the park and see bones on display at the visitor center. In addition, the Royal Tyrrell Museum in nearby Drumheller displays nearly forty full-size dinosaur skeletons. Skeletons and individual bones from the park are also on display in museums throughout the world.

In 1979 the United Nations Educational, Scientific, and Cultural Organization (UNESCO) declared Dinosaur Provincial Park to be a World Heritage Site. World Heritage Sites are places of great importance to all humanity. UNESCO tries to protect and preserve these sites for future generations.

2 Pacific Rim
NATIONAL PARK

$\mathcal{V}$ANCOUVER ISLAND IS AN ISLAND IN THE PACIFIC OCEAN. IT IS PART OF BRITISH COLUMBIA, A WESTERN CANADIAN PROVINCE. VANCOUVER IS THE LARGEST ISLAND ALONG THE WESTERN COAST OF NORTH AMERICA. IT IS ABOUT 285 MILES (460 KM) LONG AND UP TO 80 MILES (129 KM) WIDE IN SPOTS.

The island's Pacific coastline is a dangerous place for ships. In fact, sailors call the coast the Graveyard of the Pacific. Here, fierce storms can suddenly blow in from the ocean without warning. Winds can roar at more than 60 miles (100 km) per hour. They can whip up monster waves as tall as a building. Making things worse for sailors, thick fogs often reduce visibility (the distance people can see) to zero. Ships also can get caught in strong currents along the coast. These fast-flowing streams of water can grab ships and pull them onto the rocks. Since 1856 almost three hundred ships have sunk off the coast of Vancouver Island.

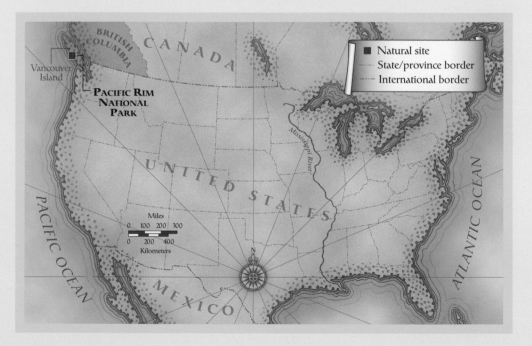

In January 1906, about 170 passengers and crew members of the *Valencia* were traveling from San Francisco, California, when the ship struck rocks off the coast of Vancouver Island. Some survivors fled the wreck in a lifeboat. They were rescued (left) by another ship. Dozens of others made it to shore. The vast majority of people, however, did not survive the shipwreck.

The *Valencia* was one of those unfortunate ships. In 1906 the *Valencia* crashed into rocks along the coast of Vancouver Island. The ship sank. Some of its passengers and crew died right away. Others clung to the ship's wreckage for two days. Rescue boats could not reach them because the water was too rough. Lifesaving crews on the shore could not reach them because there was no road to the coast through the island's dense forest.

Some people think the *Valencia*'s ghost still haunts the seashore. According to legend, on stormy days, when the ocean boils with big waves, you can see a ship fighting its way through the water. People say this "ghost ship" is the *Valencia*, searching for its dead passengers and crew.

FROM RESCUE TRAIL TO HIKING TRAIL

After the *Valencia* disaster, the government of Canada took action. The government built the Dominion Life Saving Trail through the thick forest along the coast of Vancouver Island. Rescuers used the trail to reach shipwrecks. The trail also had cabins to shelter rescuers and shipwreck survivors.

"In the name of God, where are we?"
— *Oscar Johnson, captain of the* Valencia, *after the ship hit rocks and began to sink, 1906*

GEORGE'S *Island*

Vancouver Island was named for George Vancouver. From 1792 to 1795, this British explorer mapped the Pacific coast of North America. He sailed around Vancouver Island in 1792.

By the 1940s, the rescue trail was no longer needed. By then most ships were outfitted with radar, an electronic device that helps boats (and airplanes) navigate safely, even in dense fog. The government no longer maintained the trail. It became overgrown with bushes and trees.

In 1970 the Canadian government created Pacific Rim National Park on Vancouver Island. Park workers rebuilt the lifesaving trail as a hiking trail. The trail opened for hikers in 1980. Called the West Coast Trail, the hiking trail is 48 miles (77 km) long.

An amazing view of the Pacific Ocean greets a backpacker along the West Coast Trail in Pacific Rim National Park.

The trail is only one part of a park full of wonders. Pacific Rim National Park stretches for almost 100 miles (161 km) along the southwestern coast of Vancouver Island. It extends from the town of Port Renfrew in the south to the town of Tofino farther north. In between, the park is full of lakes, rivers, beaches, forests, meadows, mountains, and valleys.

A RAIN FOREST IN CANADA?

Mention the term *rain forest*, and people often think of steamy hot places. Most rain forests are near the equator, an imaginary line around the center of Earth. Places near the equator are hot year-round and get lots of rain.

But rain forests don't just grow in hot places. Rain forests can also grow in cool climates. Any place that gets a lot of rain can have a rain forest.

A boardwalk path leads hikers through a lush, fern-filled forest in the park. Heavy rainfall along the Pacific coast creates ideal conditions for rain forests.

Mosses cover trees and vines in the rain forest in Pacific Rim National Park.

MONSTER *Trees*

The Pacific Rim National Park rain forest has some giant trees. Sitka spruces *(below)* are the largest. These trees can grow almost 300 feet (92 m) high—as tall as a thirty-story building. Some of the trees live more than one thousand years.

One of these places is the Pacific Rim National Park. The park has cool weather year-round. It also gets lots of rain—more than 10 feet (3 m) of rain each year. All that rain provides the perfect environment for a rain forest.

The rain forest in Pacific Rim National Park is a lush, green forest. It is filled with towering trees that block out the sunlight. The trees include giant spruce, western red hemlock, red cedar, and fir. Growing close to the ground are thick patches of huckleberry, salmonberry, and blueberry bushes. The ground itself is covered with a green carpet of mosses and ferns.

A Whale of a Beach

Pacific Rim National Park is famous for its beaches, which stretch for 15.5 miles (25 km) along the coast. Visitors come to the beaches to walk, jog, swim, surf, and sea kayak.

Twice a year, people can also watch gray whales swim past the beaches. Gray whales are almost the size of school buses. They can grow to be 46 feet (14 m) long and can weigh up to 72,000 pounds (32,659 kg). They live about fifty or sixty years.

In winter gray whales swim south from their feeding grounds off the coast of Alaska. They mate and give birth to their young far to the south, off the coast of western Mexico. In spring they migrate back north. Along the way, they swim past Vancouver Island. Pacific Rim National Park beaches are great spots for watching the whales as they migrate north and south each year.

Below: *A surfer totes her surfboard along a beach in the park.* Bottom: *A gray whale and her offspring swim in the calm waters near Vancouver Island.*

Above: *Sea kayakers paddle in Barkley Sound, in the Broken Group Islands.* Right: *Small creatures, such as sea stars and barnacles, line the rocks in the waters of Vancouver Island.*

BROKEN ISLANDS

Another famous part of the Pacific Rim National Park is the Broken Group Islands. Hundreds of these small islands dot a body of water called Barkley Sound. Barkley Sound is a bay, a small section of the sea that cuts into the coastline.

Unlike the sea along much of the Vancouver Island coast, the sea around the Broken Group Islands is usually calm. Because the islands are sheltered inside a bay, they do not receive high waves or fierce winds off the ocean.

By Any Other Name

Captain James Cook, a British explorer, sailed to Vancouver Island in 1778. As his ship approached the island, some indigenous (First Nations) people yelled, "Nootka, Nootka!" This term meant "come around" or "circle around" in their language. The people were telling Cook to circle around in his ship, so he could anchor in a harbor. But Cook thought they were telling him their name. The name Nootka stuck, and people used it for two hundred years. In 1978 the First Nations people of western Vancouver stopped using Nootka. They changed their name to Nuu-chah-nulth, meaning "all along the mountains and sea."

The calm sea makes the Broken Group Islands one of the park's most popular areas. Visitors can safely paddle kayaks and canoes around the islands. From the water, they can enjoy beautiful views of reefs, rocks, and coastline.

For almost four thousand years, Barkley Sound has been home to the Nuu-chah-nulth people. The Nuu-chah-nulth are a First Nations people.

A sea kayaker paddles into the sunset in Clayoquot Sound in Pacific Rim National Park.

Below: *Nuu-chah-nulth dancers would have worn this wooden gull mask during ceremonies to pray for a bountiful spring.* Bottom: *Visitors to the park walk across a stretch of beach.*

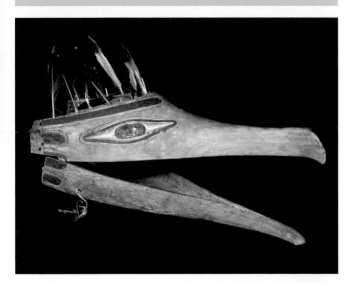

That means that their ancestors were the first people to live in this region. In earlier centuries, the Nuu-chah-nulth got their food by hunting and fishing around the Broken Group Islands.

Visitors to Vancouver Island can see beautiful totem poles created by Nuu-chah-nulth artists. These tall wooden statues are carved with images of bears, ravens, and other animals that are important in Nuu-chah-nulth culture. For instance, the bear is a symbol of power to the Nuu-chah-nulth. Nuu-chah-nulth legends say that a raven carried sunlight to Earth when the world began.

PRESERVING THE WONDER

Pacific Rim National Park is one of Canada's most popular tourist attractions. Almost one million people visit the park each year. Park rules forbid cutting down trees, constructing buildings, hunting, and other activities that would harm the plants and animals there.

3 *Redwood* FORESTS

$\mathcal{F}$ORESTS IN NORTHERN CALIFORNIA AND SOUTHERN OREGON ARE HOME TO COAST REDWOOD TREES— THE TALLEST AND SOME OF THE OLDEST LIVING THINGS IN THE WORLD. MOST COAST REDWOODS GROW TO HEIGHTS OF 200 TO 300 FEET (61 TO 91 M). THAT'S ALMOST AS TALL AS A TWENTY- OR THIRTY-STORY BUILDING. SOME COAST REDWOODS GROW EVEN HIGHER. THE TALLEST KNOWN REDWOOD, MEASURED IN 2006, WAS 378 FEET (115 M).

The trunks on these giants are enormous. Many have a diameter (width) of 22 feet (7 m). It would take about sixty people with outstretched arms to form a circle around the base of some coast redwoods. In several places, people have made "drive-through" redwoods. They've cut tunnels through the trees. Cars can drive right through them.

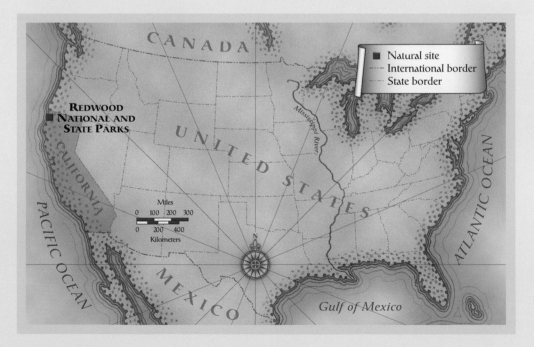

Coast redwoods grow in a strip of land about 5 to 47 miles (8 to 75 km) wide along the Pacific coast of the United States. This strip extends about 450 miles (724 km) from the Oregon–California border south to Monterey Bay, California. The cool, moist valleys in this area provide perfect conditions for redwood trees. The area gets about 100 inches (254 cm) of rain each year. Fogs often roll in from the ocean, providing more moisture for the trees and other forest plants.

OLD AS THE DINOSAURS

Redwood trees have been growing on Earth since prehistoric times. About 65 million years ago (when the last dinosaurs lived on Earth), Earth's weather was different than it is in modern times.

Right: *A car drives through a coastal redwood tree known as Chandelier Tree in Leggett, California. The hole, which is 6 feet (2 m) high by 9 feet (3 m) wide, was carved in the 1930s.* Below: *Cool mist blankets a valley in Redwood National Park.*

In the Northern Hemisphere (the section of Earth above the equator), the weather was warm year-round. The land received plenty of rainfall. The warmth and moisture provided perfect growing conditions for redwoods. Redwood trees grew in North America, Europe, Asia, and other parts of the Northern Hemisphere at this time.

A pathway meanders through towering redwoods in Muir Woods National Park, just north of San Francisco, California.

About 38 million years ago, Earth's climate got cooler and drier. Some species of redwoods could not adapt to the new climate. The trees died and their seeds no longer grew. The trees became extinct.

By about three million years ago, redwood trees had disappeared from Europe and most of Asia. Only three species of redwoods remained. These three species still grow in modern times. Dawn redwoods grow in central China. Sierra redwoods (also called giant sequoia trees) grow in central California. Coast redwoods grow on the Pacific coast of California and Oregon.

SECRET OF LIFE

Like people, trees get old, get sick, and die. Many maple trees live less than one hundred years. Oak trees live for two hundred to four hundred years. Coast redwoods live much longer—five hundred to seven hundred years. But some redwoods live even longer. The oldest known redwood was about twenty-two hundred years old.

Redwood trees live this long because of built-in protections against hazards. For instance, coast redwoods have thick bark. The bark does not burn quickly during forest fires. Redwood bark also contains bitter-tasting chemicals. These chemicals repel insects that can damage and spread diseases in other kinds of trees.

Fierce winds can easily knock down and kill many kinds of trees. But redwoods have an unusually strong network of roots. The roots spread out in the soil around each tree and then wrap around the roots of neighboring trees. This network provides an anchor beneath the ground. It keeps redwoods from blowing over in high winds.

Even with these protections, coast redwoods sometimes do burn in fires and fall over in storms. But the trees can grow again by a natural process called stump sprouting. New shoots will sprout from the base of a burned or fallen redwood tree.

OLD-TIMER

The bristlecone pine tree, which grows in California's White Mountains, lives the longest of all trees. One bristlecone pine lived to be about 4,725 years old.

Ferns, ground cover, and new trees grow on the forest floor around downed redwoods.

Above: *Giant rhododendrons bloom in Redwood National Park.* Below: *a backpacker admires the lush walls of Fern Canyon in Prairie Creek Redwoods State Park in northern California.*

REDWOOD NEIGHBORHOOD

Coast redwood forests provide a home for many other plants and animals. Some plants are giants, just like the redwoods. For instance, rhododendron bushes in redwood forests grow more than 10 feet (3 m) high. Skunk cabbage plants have leaves as long as a person's arm. Mushrooms and other fungi can reach the size of dinner plates. Giant ferns grow in a valley called Fern Canyon, in Prairie Creek Redwoods State Park in California. These plants can reach a height of more than 6 feet (2 m).

Other large trees keep the redwoods company. For instance, maple trees in the redwoods forests grow to heights of more than 80 feet (24 m). Some Douglas fir trees tower above young redwoods. Fir trees can reach heights of more than 300 feet (90 m).

Some plants and animals even live *in* the redwoods. Dead leaves and other vegetation collect in the crooks of redwoods, where tree branches meet tree trunks. The material rots and turns into rich soil.

> *"This [coast redwood forest] is the best tree-lovers monument that could possibly be found in all the forests of the world."*
>
> —U.S. conservationist John Muir, 1908

Wildflowers, wild ginger, and other plants grow in that soil—high in the sky. Thousands of birds, squirrels, chipmunks, salamanders, worms, and other animals also live in high-rise homes in the redwoods.

Many other animals, including raccoons, foxes, and hummingbirds, live in the redwood forests. Some forest animals are threatened, or in danger of becoming extinct. They include the bald eagle and northern spotted owl.

GOOD WOOD

A large coast redwood contains an enormous amount of wood—enough to build about forty one-bedroom houses. The wood is good for building. It is lightweight. It can be easily split into boards. When wet, redwood will not rot quickly like some other kinds of wood. Redwood is also beautiful. Both the bark and wood are red, which gives the trees their name.

In earlier centuries, Native Americans in California and Oregon used redwood for building homes, boats, and other objects. They rarely cut down living trees, however. Instead, Native Americans built with wood from fallen trees.

In the 1800s, many people moved to California and Oregon from the eastern United States. These newcomers began cutting down coast redwoods

A steam train hauls huge sections of a redwood tree in the early 1900s, before state and federal governments took steps to protect the mighty trees.

A Redwood in Your Backyard?

In the 1900s, many people used redwood to build fences and backyard sundecks. Redwood lasts a long time outdoors. It doesn't easily split, warp, or rot like pine and other woods. People rarely use redwood for outdoor construction anymore. It is too expensive. Instead, builders mostly use pine and other affordable wood. To preserve the wood, builders soak it in chemicals that make it resistant to rot and insects.

by the thousands. They used the wood to make houses, roof shingles, fence posts, and railroad ties.

In the 1920s, the government of California took action to protect the redwoods. It established three state parks in the redwood forests. Park rules limited the number of trees that could be cut down.

In 1968 the three state parks were combined into an area called Redwood National and State Parks. The area covers 131,983 acres (53,413 hectares). It stretches for 37 miles (60 km) along the Pacific Ocean coast. About half of all coast redwoods—including the oldest and largest redwoods—are inside the park.

People still want redwood lumber for its beauty and strength. Although it is illegal to cut redwoods in Redwood National and State Parks, people can legally cut redwoods on private land outside the park. Most of these trees are smaller and younger than the giant old trees in Redwood National and State Parks.

PROTECTING THE WONDER

Logging in the 1800s and 1900s damaged the redwood forests. With so many trees cut, large areas of the forest were left bare. In modern times, park workers have repaired much of the damage. They have planted new trees to replace those cut down. Many of the damaged areas look natural again.

In 1980 UNESCO named Redwood National and State Parks a World Heritage Site. Thousands of people from around the world visit the park each year. They marvel at the giant trees and enjoy the beautiful environment.

4 Niagara Falls

$\mathcal{W}$ATERFALLS ARE PLACES WHERE WATER IN A STREAM OR RIVER PLUNGES OVER ROCKS OR THE EDGE OF A CLIFF. IF THE STREAM IS SMALL AND THE ROCKS ARE LOW, THE WATERFALL WILL BE PEACEFUL AND SOOTHING. IF THE RIVER IS BIG AND THE CLIFF IS HIGH, THE WATERFALL WILL BE LOUD AND POWERFUL.

Of all the millions of waterfalls on Earth, Niagara Falls is one of the most famous. The falls are located on the border between New York State and Ontario, a province in eastern Canada. The water that forms the falls is the Niagara River, which flows from Lake Erie eastward to Lake Ontario. These lakes are two of the five Great Lakes—a group of large, freshwater lakes between the United States and Canada.

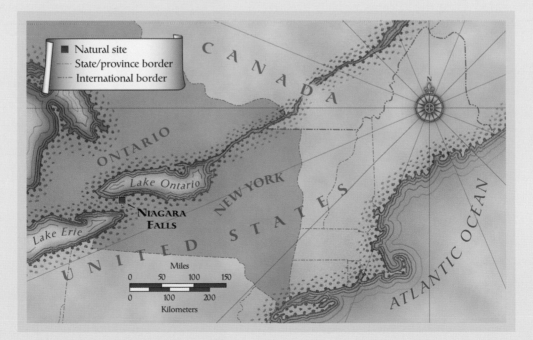

"The noise of these Falls might be heard an amazing way. I could plainly distinguish them in a calm morning more than 20 miles [32 km] away."

—U.S. explorer Jonathan Carver, 1766

The Niagara River is about 35 miles (55 km) long. As water travels along the river, it flows downhill, because Lake Erie is at a higher elevation (point above sea level) than Lake Ontario. About halfway between the two lakes, the river reaches a huge cliff called the Niagara Escarpment. When the river flows over the cliff, it forms Niagara Falls.

Niagara Falls has two main sections, the American Falls and the Horseshoe Falls. In between the two is a small island called Goat Island.

The American Falls are on the U.S. side of the border. These falls are about 1,060 feet (323 m) wide and 170 feet (52 m) high. At the American Falls, the Niagara River drops in a long straight sheet. A smaller falls called Bridal Veil Falls is also on the U.S. side. It is separated from the American Falls by tiny Luna Island.

The Horseshoe Falls are on the Canadian side of the border. These falls are U shaped instead of straight. That shape gives the falls their name. About 2,600 feet (792 m) wide and 176 feet (54 m) high, the Horseshoe Falls are much larger than the American Falls. The Horseshoe Falls carry about nine times more water.

Niagara Falls makes a thunderous roar. The gigantic sheets of falling water sound like a thousand motorcycles. People can hear the rumble of the water far away. Spray and mist fill the air above the falls. Sunlight shining on the mist sometimes forms gigantic rainbows.

HONEYMOON Capital

Niagara Falls is called the Honeymoon Capital of the World. That tradition started in the early 1800s, when famous people began traveling to the falls for honeymoons. The early honeymooners included Jérôme Bonaparte and his bride in 1804. (Bonaparte was the brother of famous French emperor Napoléon Bonaparte.)

Above: *Tour boats carry visitors up the Niagara River to enjoy an up-close look at the American Falls on the left and Horseshoe Falls, in Canada, to the right.* Bottom left: *Sunlight hitting the mist above the falls creates a rainbow.* Bottom right: *An overhead view of Horseshoe Falls*

NATURAL HISTORY

The story of Niagara Falls starts during the last Ice Age, which began about two million years ago. At that time, enormous glaciers, or ice sheets, moved across North America and other places on Earth. As they moved, the glaciers picked up huge rocks, sort of like snowballs rolling over dirt. The rocks scraped the land like bulldozers, carving out huge grooves and craters.

About ten thousand years ago, Earth's climate warmed and the glaciers melted. The craters and grooves filled with water from the melting glaciers. In North America, some of these craters and grooves became the Great Lakes, the Niagara River, and Niagara Falls.

LOCATION, LOCATION, LOCATION

Other waterfalls are higher and wider than Niagara Falls and carry much more water. For instance, Angel Falls in the South American country of Venezuela is

Toronto, Ontario (below, right), overlooks Niagara Falls from the north. The U.S. city of Buffalo, New York, lies to the south.

3,212 feet (979 m) high. It is the world's highest waterfall. Livingstone Falls on Africa's Congo River carries almost twelve times more water than Niagara Falls.

Still, Niagara Falls is more famous than these other falls. Perhaps that's because of its location. Niagara Falls is near the big U.S. city of Buffalo, New York, and the big Canadian city of Toronto, Ontario. Millions of people live close enough to drive to the falls on vacation. Airports also are close by, so people from around the world can easily fly to see this wonder. Plenty of nearby hotels have rooms for tourists. Restaurants offer good food. Angel Falls and Livingstone Falls, on the other hand, are in very remote parts of the world. They are far from big cities. It is difficult and expensive for tourists to go there.

STUNTS AND SPECTACLES

Over the years, people have staged many stunts at Niagara Falls. For instance, in 1827 hotel owners attracted tourists by sending an old ship over the falls. The ship smashed into rocks above the falls and broke into pieces. Those pieces then plunged over the falls.

In the summer of 1859, French tightrope walker Jean François Gravelot walked across the American Falls on a tightrope. Known as the Great Blondin, Gravelot walked on a rope 3 inches (8 cm) in diameter and 1,100 feet (335 m) long. As thousands of people watched, Blondin took step after step, completing the walk in about twenty minutes. Blondin carried a long pole to help him balance. Later in the summer, he repeated the walk eight more times. The most amazing walk was on August 14, when Blondin carried a man on his back.

In 1859 and 1860, Jean François "the Great Blondin" Gravelot navigated a tightrope above the American Falls. This picture shows Blondin carrying his manager on his back.

The next summer, Blondin returned and performed the stunt again and again.

In 1901 a schoolteacher named Annie Taylor had herself sealed into a specially built wooden barrel. Helpers dropped the barrel into the Niagara River, and over the Horseshoe Falls went Taylor. Crew members on a boat waiting below the falls rescued the barrel. Amazingly, Taylor was still alive, although she was bloody and bruised.

Later in the 1900s, other people tried to repeat Taylor's stunt. A few survived unharmed. Others drowned, were smashed by rocks and killed, or were badly hurt. In modern times, anyone who tries such a stunt (and lives) will be arrested.

Left: *Annie Taylor prepares to leave the shore before her daring feat of traveling over the falls in a wooden barrel.* **Right:** *A shaken Taylor climbs back to shore after surviving her stunt.*

"Niagara was at once stamped upon my heart, an Image of Beauty; to remain there, changeless and indelible [unforgettable], until its pulses cease to beat, for ever."
—*British writer Charles Dickens, 1842*

Dams on the Niagara River provide power for creating electricity for millions of homes.

WATERPOWER

For thousands of years, people have known that water flowing over a large waterfall can be a good source of power. In the 1700s, engineers dug channels that diverted the Niagara River's water to flow over paddle wheels. Those spinning wheels powered machinery at sawmills (for cutting logs) and flour mills (for grinding flour).

In the late 1800s, people started using the Niagara River to create electricity. They used the river's flow to turn engines called turbines. The spinning turbines generated electricity. Electricity created by the power of flowing water is called hydroelectricity.

In modern times, two hydroelectric power stations operate near Niagara Falls. These stations produce electricity for millions of people in the United States and Canada. The stations divert between 50 and 75 percent of the Niagara River's water before it reaches the falls. After the water passes through turbines at the power stations, it returns to the river below the falls.

WORRIES ABOUT THE WONDER

Diverting water from Niagara Falls is both negative and positive. On the negative side, diverting water makes the falls smaller and less spectacular. If the falls get too small, people won't want to come see them. That would hurt businesses that rely on tourists. For this reason, the United States and Canada have signed a treaty regulating the amount of water that flows over the falls.

The treaty allows the most water to flow in the summer and during the daytime—when most tourists are visiting.

On the positive side, water diversion provides people with much-needed electricity. And water diversion actually helps preserve Niagara Falls. Here's how: As water plunges over the falls, it erodes (wears away) rock at the edge of the Niagara Escarpment. As the rock wears away, Niagara Falls moves farther and farther back up the Niagara River. In the early 1900s, Horseshoe Falls was receding (moving back) at a rate of more than 3 feet (1 m) per year.

ROCKY *River*

The erosion at Niagara Falls usually happens slowly, with rock wearing away a little at a time. Sometimes, however, rock breaks off in big chunks. For instance, in 1954 a big piece of rock broke off the American Falls and fell into the river below. The big rock is still visible below the falls.

Tourists at the American Falls watch as millions of gallons of water hurtle over the Niagara Escarpment, creating the natural beauty of Niagara Falls. Between all the waterfalls, 45 million gallons (170 million liters) of water rush over the edge per minute.

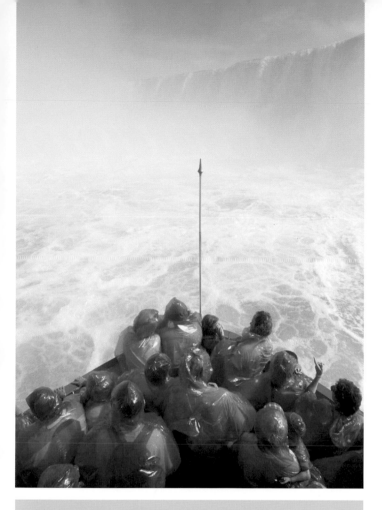

Passengers on the Maid of the Mist *get up close and personal with the falls.*

By diverting water and regulating water flow, people have been able to slow the erosion. In the 2000s, Horseshoe Falls recedes only about 1.2 inches (3 cm) each year.

The erosion is slow, but eventually Niagara Falls will disappear. Rock will continue to wear away until the falls reach Lake Erie. In about fifty thousand years, the spectacular waterfall wonder could be completely gone.

For the time being, however, people can still enjoy Niagara Falls. Both New York and Ontario have established parks around the falls. New York's Niagara Reservation State Park includes the American Falls and the Bridal Veil Falls. Ontario's Queen Victoria Park includes the Horseshoe Falls.

The parks have many activities for visitors. Boat rides are among the most popular. Passengers wearing raincoats ride on boats called *Maid of the Mist*. The boats travel right below the falls. Without raincoats, passengers would be drenched in spray from the falling water.

THE REAL
Maid of the Mist

The *Maid of the Mist* passenger boats were named for an ancient Iroquois legend. It told of a beautiful young woman swept to her death over Niagara Falls. People later said they could see her face in the mist swirling around the falls.

5 THE Grand Canyon

$\mathcal{E}$ARLY EXPLORERS IN THE AMERICAN

WEST GREATLY FEARED A HUGE CANYON IN NORTHWESTERN ARIZONA.

EXPLORERS WHO VISITED THE CANYON IN THE 1800S TOLD TERRIFYING

STORIES. ONE EXPLORER CALLED THE CANYON THE GATES OF HELL.

A mighty river, then named the Grand River, flowed through the bottom of the canyon. Explorers described monstrous waterfalls on the river. In these spots, the river suddenly spilled over the tops of cliffs. People in boats on the river could not see the waterfalls until they were right at their edges. The people had no time to save themselves. Their boats tumbled over the falls and smashed on the rocks below. Other stories told of powerful whirlpools. In these spots, the river water swirled in a circle. Anything caught in a whirlpool would be sucked below the surface. The river also had terrifying rapids, areas where water rushes and foams over huge rocks. Boats sailing into the rapids were often smashed to pieces.

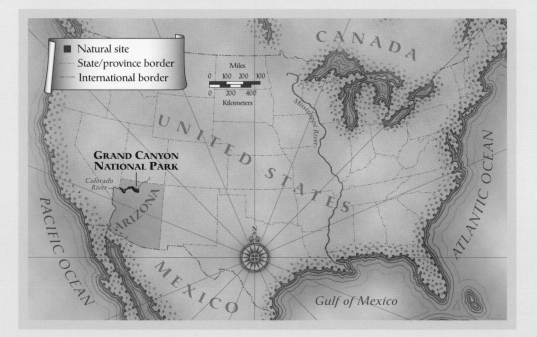

Most people thought it was impossible to sail down the river and explore the canyon. Finally, in 1869 an American explorer named John Wesley Powell (who had lost part of one arm during the Civil War of 1861–1865) led an expedition down the river and through the canyon. His adventure made people aware of a breathtaking natural wonder that he named the Grand Canyon.

John Wesley Powell took nine men in four boats down the Colorado River in 1869.

GRAND INDEED

The Grand Canyon is grand in size and beauty. It extends for about 277 miles (446 km) through Arizona. The canyon is more than 1 mile (1.6 km) deep in some places. Its width ranges from 4 to 18 miles (6.4 to 29 km).

Layers of rock in the canyon create a rainbow of colors. The bottom layer is black. The next layer up gleams brilliant red. Other layers are yellow, brown, green, lavender, and pink. The shades change with the changing light of the desert sun.

Thick forests of oak trees, blue spruce, Ponderosa pine, and other trees cover the landscape around the canyon's rim. Small piñon pines and juniper bushes grow on high cliffs inside the canyon. The canyon floor is a dry desert with only a few bushes. Many animals live in and around the canyon. The largest animals include mountain lions, bobcats, bighorn sheep, mule deer, and coyotes.

Rushing through the canyon floor is the river that frightened explorers more than one hundred years ago. In modern times, it is called the Colorado River. This mighty river begins in the Rocky Mountains of northern Colorado.

"The sun is going down and the shadows are settling in the [canyon]. The [red] gleams and rosy hues, the green and gray tints are changing to [somber] brown above, and black shadows below."

—Explorer John Wesley Powell, 1869

A photograph taken at sunset from Mohave Point, on the South Rim of the Grand Canyon, highlights the beautiful colors of the rock layers.

It flows southwest for 1,450 miles (2,330 km) into the Gulf of California, part of the Pacific Ocean.

CARVING A CANYON

Most canyons, including the Grand Canyon, are carved out of the ground by rivers. As its flows, a river picks up loose soil that sits along its banks and on its bottom. Over time, more and more soil washes away with the river. The river cuts deeper and deeper into the ground. The canyon gets wider and wider.

In the case of the Grand Canyon, much of this digging happened during spring floods. In May and June, water from snow melting in the Rocky Mountains poured into the Colorado River. The river swelled and overflowed its banks in great floods. The roaring floodwaters chewed away the soil and rock surrounding the river with tremendous force. The water even picked up rocks the size of cars. Such big rocks tumbling through the water banged against cliffs and tore away even more soil and rock.

Frozen water also enlarged the canyon. Rainwater seeped into cracks in soil and rock along the rim of the canyon. In cold weather, the water froze, becoming ice. The ice expanded inside the cracks. The pressure forced big pieces

THE MIGHTY *Colorado*

The Colorado River brings life to the southwestern United States and northwestern Mexico. It is the main source of water for 25 million people. The Colorado also provides water to 1 million acres (400,000 hectares) of farmland. People throughout the United States eat fruits and vegetables grown on that land.

An aerial view of the Grand Canyon shows where the Colorado River has carved out winding channels in the rock, leaving behind an impressive sight.

of the canyon walls to break off. They fell into the river below.

As big rocks tumbled down, they sometimes hit other rocks and broke them loose from the canyon walls. The falling rocks sometimes became a landslide. Huge chunks of rock and soil came sliding down, widening the canyon even more.

The process of forming the Grand Canyon has taken six million years. And it's still in progress. As the Colorado River rushes through the canyon, its waters keep carving away at the canyon walls, making the canyon even larger.

A STORYBOOK IN THE CANYON

The Grand Canyon is like a storybook of Earth's history. At the very bottom of the canyon are some of the oldest rocks visible on Earth. These rocks are almost two billion years old. (Earth is about five billion years old.)

Scientists think that the rocks at the bottom of the canyon were once the base of a big mountain range. The mountains may have been as tall as Mount Everest, the world's highest mountain. Over millions of years, water, wind, and ice wore down these mountains. The land became a flat plain. Then, about one billion years ago, a second mountain range formed. Eventually, that second mountain range was also worn away by water and weather.

After the second mountain range eroded, Earth's climate went through several warm periods and cool periods. When the climate warmed, big sheets of ice melted. Sea levels on Earth rose. Water flooded in from the ocean, creating a sea over the Grand Canyon region. During cool periods, water froze again into huge ice sheets. Sea levels fell. Water retreated from the Grand Canyon region, leaving dry land.

This process of warming and cooling happened several times. Each time water covered the Grand Canyon region, sediments built up on the seafloor. These deposits included dead plants and the shells of sea animals. Eventually, the sediment hardened into layers of rock.

OTHER *Grand Canyons*

Several other canyons are also called the Grand Canyon. Yellowstone National Park has a Grand Canyon. So does the state of Pennsylvania. Canada has three Grand Canyons. Another grand canyon, the Grand Canyon du Verdon, is in southeastern France.

Over six million years, the Colorado River cut through the sediment, exposing the different layers of rock. The layers are evidence of the ancient mountains and seas that once covered the Grand Canyon. The rocks contain remains of prehistoric plants and animals. The layers have helped scientists understand Earth's early history.

PEOPLE OF THE CANYON

Many groups of people have lived in the Grand Canyon. The first were Paleo-Indians—the ancestors of modern-day Native Americans. These residents moved into the area around the Grand Canyon about eleven thousand years ago. They hunted animals and gathered wild plants for food. In later centuries, various Native American groups lived in and near the canyon. These groups included the Hopi, Zuni, Paiute, Havasupai, and Navajo.

In 1540 Spanish explorer García López de Cárdenas became the first

"The one great sight which every American should see."
—*U.S. president Theodore Roosevelt, describing the Grand Canyon, 1903*

European to see the Grand Canyon. He was traveling with an expedition led by Francisco Vásquez de Coronado, a more famous Spanish explorer. John Wesley Powell's 1869 expedition was the first to explore the full length of the canyon. In 1871 Powell led another expedition to the canyon. On this journey, he made the first map of the Grand Canyon. In 1919 the U.S. government made the Grand Canyon into a national park.

WORRIES ABOUT THE WONDER

For millions of years, melting snow from the Rocky Mountains poured into the Colorado River every spring. The extra water turned the Colorado into the raging river that John Wesley Powell and other explorers feared in the 1800s. The fast-moving water cleaned weeds, rocks, and wood off sandbars along the riverbanks. When the water receded, it left a fresh, clean layer of sand along the riverbanks. The clean sandbars provided healthy homes for fish and plants.

But in the mid-1900s, people changed the flow of the Colorado River. In 1963 workers completed the Glen Canyon Dam in Utah, north of the canyon. This dam holds back the Colorado River before it reaches the Grand Canyon. The backed-up water forms a lake called Lake Powell (named for John Wesley Powell).

The 710-foot-high (216 m) Glen Canyon Dam controls the flow of the Colorado River upstream from the Grand Canyon. Although the dam provides hydroelectric power and water to the Southwest, scientists worry that it hurts the environment.

The dam offers many benefits. It has hydroelectric turbines that create electricity. Lake Powell stores valuable water that people use in their homes and to water crops. People enjoy boating, swimming, and fishing at the lake.

But damming the Colorado also hurts the river. Engineers release water through the dam gradually. They do not allow the Colorado to turn into a raging river each spring. Without spring floods, the river cannot create new, clean sandbars. Since the dam was built, four fish species that once lived around the sandbars have gone extinct. Two other species are in danger of extinction.

In 1996, 2004, and 2008, engineers tried to correct the situation. They cleaned the canyon by releasing extra water from the dam. For more than two days each time, the water roared down the Colorado as it had in earlier centuries. Like a huge fire hose, the rushing water cleaned the riverbanks and created fresh new sandbars. Scientists are waiting to see if fish populations will increase as a result of the three "spring cleanings."

Bottom: *River rafters brave the rapids during a trip down the Colorado.* Below: *Rafters have pulled over for a closer look at Deer Creek Falls.*

GRAND CANYON NATIONAL PARK

Grand Canyon National Park stretches for 290 miles (467 km) along the Colorado River. It contains the canyon itself as well as lands around the rim. It is one of the most popular parks in the United States. More than five million people visit each year.

Visitors to the park camp, hike, and enjoy the spectacular scenery. Some people take rafting trips on the Colorado River. Others hike down into the canyon and back up. Visitors can also ride into the canyon on mules. In 1979 UNESCO designated the canyon as a World Heritage Site.

Yellowstone
National Park

*I*N THE LATE 1800s, EXPLORERS TOLD FANTASTIC STORIES ABOUT THE YELLOWSTONE RIVER VALLEY IN WYOMING. THE EXPLORERS CLAIMED THAT THE VALLEY HAD POOLS OF MUD THAT BUBBLED AND BOILED LIKE A WITCH'S KETTLE. THEY TOLD ABOUT POOLS OF BLACK, YELLOW, BLUE, AND GREEN WATER. THEY DESCRIBED FOUNTAINS OF STEAMING HOT WATER THAT SPOUTED HIGH INTO THE AIR. THEY TOLD STORIES ABOUT BEAUTIFUL HIDDEN CANYONS WITH RAINBOW-COLORED ROCKS INSIDE. THEY SAID THE ROCKS WERE LAYERED LIKE A STACK OF PANCAKES. THEY SAID THE LAYERS GLOWED IN THE SUNLIGHT IN SHADES OF RED, YELLOW, AND ORANGE.

"We came into [Yellowstone] . . . and immediately found ourselves in the midst of the wonders of this enchanted land. The boiling springs and geysers were all around us, and, accustomed as we were to the marvels of Western scenery, we hardly knew what to think of the phenomena."
—John C. Davis, a member of an 1864 expedition to Yellowstone

Some people in the eastern United States didn't believe the stories. They sounded too fantastic to be true. During this era, the Yellowstone River valley was part of the Wild West. Only Native Americans and a few white settlers lived in this area. Very few Americans from the East had seen the wonders of the valley up close.

In 1871 William Henry Jackson, a photographer and explorer, took pictures of the Yellowstone River valley. The photographs convinced people back east that the valley was a land of natural wonders.

In Washington, D.C., members of Congress saw Jackson's photos. They decided that the Yellowstone River valley should be protected and preserved for all Americans to enjoy. In 1872 the U.S. government made Yellowstone the world's first national park.

William Henry Jackson photographed the crater of the soon-to-be-famous Old Faithful geyser in 1871.

PARK OF WONDERS

Yellowstone National Park is named for the Yellowstone River, which flows through the area. In earlier eras, the Minnetaree Indians called the river Mi tsi a-da-zi, which means "Yellow Rock River." The name came from the area's yellow cliffs and rocks. English-speaking trappers, who hunted the region's animals for their valuable furs, later translated the name into English: Yellowstone.

Yellowstone is an enormous park. It covers more than 2 million acres (809,400 hectares). It is larger than the states of Rhode Island and Delaware combined. About 96 percent of the park's land is in Wyoming. The rest is in Montana to the north and Idaho to the west

The park includes mountain ranges, forests, grasslands, and canyons. The park even has its own Grand Canyon, called the Grand Canyon of the Yellowstone. The Yellowstone River carved out this canyon over millions of years. The canyon reaches a depth of 900 feet (275 m) in some places. At its widest, it is 0.5 mile (0.8 km) across.

Several rivers, including the Yellowstone River, flow through the park. Together these rivers contain about three hundred spectacular waterfalls. Yellowstone Lake is the park's largest body of water. The lake covers 136 square miles (352 sq. km). It is up to 400 feet (122 m) deep in spots and has 110 miles (177 km) of shoreline.

The Yellowstone River roars over Yellowstone Falls and enters the Grand Canyon of Yellowstone. The steep hillsides are made of the yellow rock that gave the park its name.

The Yellowstone River flows out of Yellowstone Lake.

Yellowstone Lake fills the bowl-shaped crater of the Yellowstone Super Volcano. A volcano is an opening in Earth's surface. Sometimes, hot ash, gases, and rocks erupt through the opening. Scientists say that the Yellowstone Super Volcano is an active volcano. That means it might erupt in the future.

HOT AND BUBBLY

Yellowstone National Park sits on what scientists call a hot spot. At hot spots, magma—red-hot melted rock from deep below the ground—rises up toward Earth's surface.

YELLOWSTONE VOLCANO
Another Eruption?

The Yellowstone Super Volcano erupts about once every 600,000 years. The last eruption was 640,000 years ago, so the volcano is overdue for an eruption. Hot lava, ash, and gas from the last eruption destroyed everything for hundreds of miles around. If the volcano erupts again, it could do similar damage.

Old Faithful blasts steaming hot water out of its crater approximately every seventy-six minutes.

Heat from magma creates some of Yellowstone's greatest wonders.

One of these wonders is Old Faithful. Old Faithful is a geyser. Geysers are hot springs that occasionally shoot jets of steam and hot water into the air. Geysers form when water from Earth's surface seeps down into areas with magma. Heat from the magma turns some of the water into steam. The steam rises up. It pushes against the water above it. The heated water finally shoots into the air in a tall jet.

Old Faithful got its name because it erupts so regularly. About every seventy-six minutes, it shoots a spout of water about 170 feet (50 m) into the air. The eruptions last for up to five minutes at a time.

Yellowstone has about two hundred other geysers. Some are more spectacular than Old Faithful. A geyser called the Giant, for instance, sends a spout of water 200 feet (60 m) into the air. Another geyser, the Giantess, erupts for more than four hours at a time. Steamboat Geyser, the world's tallest geyser, spouts as high as 380 feet (120 m). However, these geysers do not erupt as often or as regularly as Old Faithful.

Hot magma below the surface creates other wonders in Yellowstone. For instance, the park has bubbling pools of mud called mud pots. They form when steam and gases hiss up from below the ground. They turn the soil on the ground into bubbling mud. Some of the mud pots are 30 feet (9 m) in diameter. Yellowstone also has fumaroles, or steam vents.

GREAT *Geysers*

Iceland, an island nation in the North Atlantic Ocean, has more than two hundred geysers. Iceland's most famous geyser is called Geysir, or the Great Geysir. It is the first geyser to be mentioned in written history. The word *geyser* comes from *gjósa*, which means "to erupt" in the Icelandic language.

A mud pot bubbles and steams in the West Thumb Geyser Basin. Winter snow lies all around.

These are spots where steam and gases hiss and roar out of the ground.

Yellowstone has thousands of hot springs. At hot springs, hot water seeps up to Earth's surface and forms pools. As the water evaporates (dries up), it leaves behind minerals that pile up into unusual shapes. At Mammoth Hot Springs in Yellowstone, the minerals have formed piles up to 300 feet (90 m) high.

LIFE IN YELLOWSTONE

An amazing variety of living things make their homes in Yellowstone National Park. Some of the smallest residents are algae. These microscopic plants grow in hot springs. Algae give some hot springs the amazing colors that explorers told about in the 1800s. One spring in Yellowstone is blue, green, and orange. It is named Morning Glory Pool because it resembles a colorful morning glory flower.

Above: *Bison and elk at Firehole River*
Right: *Bighorn sheep at Lamar River*

Yellowstone is also home to more than three hundred species of animals. They include grizzly bears, buffalo, wolves, coyotes, moose, elks, deer, antelopes, bighorn sheep, whooping cranes, and bald eagles.

Over the centuries, many groups of Native Americans have lived in Yellowstone. The first were Paleo-Indians. They fished and hunted in the area about eleven thousand years ago. Later, Native American peoples, including the Bannock, the Crow, and the Blackfoot, also hunted in Yellowstone. Some Native Americans came to Yellowstone to collect obsidian, a dark, glassy rock.

"For my own part I almost wished I could spend the remainder of my days in a place like this where happiness and contentment seemed to reign in wild romantic splendor."

—U.S. explorer Osborne Russell, 1835

Native peoples used obsidian to make razor-sharp knives, arrowheads, and other weapons.

The first white person to see Yellowstone was John Colter. He was a member of the Lewis and Clark expedition. Led by Meriwether Lewis and William Clark, this U.S. government expedition explored the American West from 1804 to 1806. Lewis and Clark never visited Yellowstone themselves. Colter traveled there alone in 1807, after the other members of the expedition had returned home.

PROTECTING THE WONDER

Yellowstone National Park is a UNESCO World Heritage Site. It is a popular tourist attraction. Almost three million people visit the park each year. Some travelers come to the park from outside the United States.

People have damaged parts of Yellowstone. In 1988 a smoker threw down a cigarette without putting it out completely. The cigarette started a fire that burned almost 15 percent of the park. Over the years, other people threw coins, sticks, and trash into Morning Glory Pool. The objects plugged the spring that fed the pool. As a result, the pool got cooler. Some of its colorful algae died.

Most tourists, however, enjoy this natural wonder without damaging it. Visitors to Yellowstone marvel at Old Faithful, hot springs, and other wonders. Many visitors drive through the park and stop their cars at famous sights. Others hike on trails, backpack into remote areas of the park, and pitch tents in campgrounds. Visitors can also go horseback riding, boating, and fishing in Yellowstone National Park.

ONE WARM FEBRUARY AFTERNOON IN 1943, DIONISIO PULIDO WAS WORKING PEACEFULLY ON HIS FARM NEAR PARICUTÍN. THIS TINY VILLAGE WAS IN THE CENTRAL MEXICAN STATE OF MICHOACÁN. IT WAS ABOUT 200 MILES (322 KM) WEST OF MEXICO CITY, THE CAPITAL OF MEXICO.

Suddenly, Pulido stopped his work and stood up straight with fright. His eyes grew wide, and his jaw dropped in amazement. The ground under Pulido's feet had begun to shake. A sound like thunder rumbled across his cornfield. He could feel the rumble in his chest as a crack opened in the ground nearby.

The ground around the crack began to swell like a balloon. Smoke and ashes hissed out of the crack. Pulido staggered to his horse and galloped away from the terrifying scene. Pulido had been an eyewitness to the birth of the Paricutín Volcano.

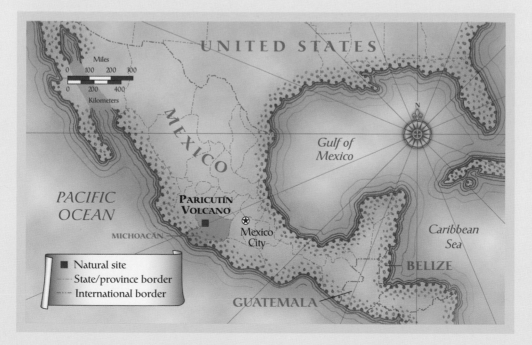

GROWING UP—FAST

When volcanoes erupt, they release hot ashes, gases, and red-hot melted rock into the air. Afterward, the rock and ashes cool, harden, and pile up around the opening. They form a cone-shaped mountain around the center of the volcano.

It may take thousands or millions of years for a mountain to build up around a volcano. But Paricutín grew faster than the bean stalk in the story of "Jack and the Beanstalk." Scientists think that Paricutín was the fastest-growing volcano in all Earth's history.

By the end of the first day of eruptions, the mountain around the volcano was about 6 feet (2 m) tall. Six days later, the mountain was as high as a fifteen-story building. Paricutín erupted nonstop for the next nine years. When it stopped erupting in February 1952, it was one big nine-year-old. Paricutín had grown to a height of 10,400 feet (3,170 m). Its base was large enough to cover ten thousand high school football fields.

PARICUTÍN DESTROYS PARICUTÍN

Volcanic eruptions can be frightening and destructive. During volcanoes, lava and hot gases shoot into the air like fountains of fire. Volcanic eruptions may contain red-hot rocks as big as watermelons. Lava from volcanoes can set buildings on fire.

Above: *Paricutín erupted from a Mexican field on February 21, 1943*. Below: *Paricutín on February 22, 1943*

Lava flows from Paracutín on March 5, 1943.

It can bury buildings, trees, and other objects. In addition, as magma shoots up from underground, it may cause an earthquake. That shaking of the earth can do additional damage. It can knock down buildings, break power lines, and start fires.

During Paricutín's eruptions, blasts of lava and glowing rocks flew more than 1,000 feet (305 m) into the air. Lava from Paricutín quickly covered Dionisio Pulido's cornfields. On June 12, 1943, a river of lava began flowing toward the village of Paricutín. The next day, people began evacuating, or leaving, the village. They moved in with relatives and friends in nearby villages.

"I felt a thunder, the trees trembled, and . . . it was then I saw how, in the hole, the ground swelled and raised itself 2 or 2.5 meters [6.6 to 8 feet] high, and a kind of smoke or fine dust—grey, like ashes—began to rise up in a portion of the crack that I had not previously seen. . . . Immediately more smoke began to rise with a hiss or whistle, loud and continuous; and there was a smell of sulfur."

—Dionisio Pulido, describing the birth of Paricutín, 1943

The lava piled up, set Paricutín's buildings on fire, and buried the village. Then lava flowed toward the larger village of San Juan Parangaricutiro. That village was also evacuated. People in both villages lost their homes, but no one died.

EYEWITNESSES

When Paricutín began to erupt, the news spread fast. Scientists rarely have a chance to see the creation of a volcano. So scientists from around the world were eager to watch the eruptions. By watching Paricutín, scientists learned how volcanoes form, grow, and change the surrounding land.

Tourists also began arriving soon after the volcano's birth. From a safe distance, people watched the volcano erupt. They saw giant sparks of red-hot lava splatter into the air. They heard loud booms as glowing rocks shot out of the volcano. It was like a spectacular fireworks display on the Fourth of July.

INGREDIENTS FOR ERUPTION

Volcanoes begin more than 30 miles (48 km) below Earth's surface. In that area, the temperature is about 2,730°F (1,500°C). At that temperature, rock melts into magma, a thick, cherry red liquid.

Sometimes, magma rises up toward Earth's surface. The heat of the magma melts the surrounding rocks, leaving empty chambers below ground. Magma pours into these chambers. As more magma pours in, the pressure builds up like water in a water balloon. If the pressure gets high enough, magma bursts out onto Earth's surface. Once magma erupts onto the surface, it is called lava.

VOLCANO COUNTRY

Earth's crust, or outer shell, is not solid. It is broken into seven big plates, or slabs of rock. Scientists call these slabs tectonic plates. The plates are up to 50 miles (81 km) thick. The smallest plate is 1,400 miles (2,000 km) from one side to the other. The largest is almost 9,000 miles (14,000 km) wide—bigger than Earth's biggest continent! The plates float on magma, almost like leaves floating in a puddle of water.

The tectonic plates move constantly. In some places, the plates slowly move away from one another. In other places, one plate might sink below another. When one tectonic plate slides below another, magma can easily rise toward Earth's surface, creating volcanoes. The Paricutín Volcano formed when the Pacific Plate sank below the North American Plate.

Paricutín is in an area famous for its volcanoes. Called the Trans-Mexican Volcanic Belt, this region stretches about 700 miles (1,127 km) across southern

Molten rock explodes out of Paricutín and pours down its sides in this photo at night, taken in 1947.

"Paricutín has provided scientists with a unique opportunity for study, as it is the first volcano they have been able to examine from the moment of its 'birth.'"

—New York Times *reporter Sidney Gruson, 1962*

Mexico. For millions of years, volcanic eruptions have filled the area with thick layers of hardened lava. In some places, the lava is almost 6,000 feet (1,829 m) thick. Over hundreds of years, lava from a volcanic eruption breaks down into small pieces. It gradually becomes rich soil that is good for growing crops.

In modern times, only two volcanoes have erupted in the Mexican Volcanic Belt. The Paricutín Volcano is one of them. The other is the El Jorullo Volcano, about 50 miles (81 km) southeast of Paricutín. El Jorullo formed in 1759. In the first six weeks, it grew to a height of 820 feet (250 m). The volcano erupted for fifteen years. It destroyed rich farmland, covering the earth with lava and ash. When the eruption ended in 1774, El Jorullo was 4,331 feet (1,320 m) high.

PEOPLE AND PARICUTÍN

Prehistoric people began settling around the Trans-Mexican Volcanic Belt almost ten thousand years ago. The region had dense forests that provided people with wood for building, and plants and animals for food. Because of past volcanic eruptions, the region had rich, fertile soil. Moist air from the Pacific Ocean also brought lots of rain. The combination of fertile soil and plentiful rainfall made the Trans-Mexican Volcanic Belt a region of excellent farmland.

The ancient Aztec people founded a great empire in the area in the A.D. 1300s. Spanish explorer Hernán Cortés conquered the Aztec Empire in 1521. Afterward, more Spanish people moved to the area. In modern times, many Tarascan Indian people live near the Paricutín Volcano.

Scientists think that volcanoes in the Trans-Mexican Volcanic Belt may erupt in the future, although they do not know whether or not Paricutín will erupt again. Even though Paricutín no longer erupts, thousands of tourists still visit it each year. They marvel at the giant cone-shaped mountain that grew in a cornfield. In some places, visitors walk over black lava that has hardened into rock. In other places, thick layers of black, volcanic dust cover the land.

Visitors also enjoy the beautiful countryside that Paricutín did not damage. Michoacán has mountains, valleys, lakes, waterfalls, and lovely beaches. Tourists enjoy camping, hiking, and other outdoor activities there.

The church in San Juan Parangaricutiro is embedded in lava rock.

UNDER *the Lava*

The church tower of San Juan Parangaricutiro is practically the only trace of the two villages destroyed by Paricutín. During the eruption, lava flowed around the church and poured through its doors and windows. It covered the building almost to the roof. But the church remained standing. In the twenty-first century, the church tower rises above a black sea of lava. Buried below the lava are old houses and other buildings.

TIMELINE

1540   García López de Cárdenas, a Spanish explorer, becomes the first European to see the Grand Canyon.

1759   El Jorullo Volcano erupts in Mexico. It continues erupting for another fifteen years.

1792   British explorer George Vancouver explores Vancouver Island, which is later named in his honor.

1859   The Great Blondin walks across Niagara Falls on a tightrope. He repeats the stunt many more times, once even carrying a man on his back.

1869   U.S. explorer John Wesley Powell leads this first expedition through the Grand Canyon.

1871   During a U.S. government expedition, William Henry Jackson takes the first photographs of the Yellowstone River valley.

1872   U.S. Congress creates Yellowstone National Park.

1884   Joseph Tyrrell discovers the skull of *Albertosaurus* on the Red Deer River in Alberta, Canada.

1901   Schoolteacher Annie Taylor is the first person to float over Niagara Falls in a barrel. She survives with only minor injuries.

1906   The *Valencia* sinks off the coast of Vancouver Island.

1910s   Paleontologists Barnum Brown and Charles Sternberg dig for dinosaur bones along the Red Deer River in Alberta.

1919   The U.S. government creates Grand Canyon National Park in northwestern Arizona.

1943   Paricutín Volcano begins to form in Michoacán, Mexico.

1950   The United States and Canada sign a treaty regulating the amount of water that flows across Niagara Falls.

1952   The Paricutín Volcano stops erupting.

1955   Canada creates Dinosaur Provincial Park in Alberta. Only scientists are allowed to dig for bones in the park.

1963   The Glen Canyon Dam across the Colorado River is completed. Lake Powell forms behind the dam.

1968   California combines three state parks to create Redwood National and State Parks.

1970   Canada creates the Pacific Rim National Park on Vancouver Island.

1978   Yellowstone National Park becomes a World Heritage Site.

1979 Dinosaur Provincial Park becomes a World Heritage Site. The Grand Canyon becomes a World Heritage Site.

1980 The West Coast Trail opens in Pacific Rim National Park. Redwood National and State Parks becomes a World Heritage Site.

1988 A fire started by a cast-off cigarette burns about 15 percent of Yellowstone National Park.

2008 To create clean sandbars in the Grand Canyon, engineers release extra water from the Glen Canyon Dam (a procedure also carried out in 1996 and 2004).

CHOOSE AN EIGHTH WONDER

Now that you've read about the seven natural wonders of North America, do a little research to choose an eighth wonder. You may enjoy working with a friend.

To do your research, look at some of the websites and books listed on pages 76 and 77. Look for places in North America that

- *are especially large*
- *are exceptionally beautiful*
- *were unknown to foreigners for many centuries*
- *are unlike any other place on Earth*

You might even try gathering photos and writing your own chapter on the eighth wonder!

GLOSSARY AND PRONUNCIATION GUIDE

continents: the seven giant landmasses on Earth. The continents are Africa, Antarctica, Asia, Australia, Europe, North America, and South America.

erode: to wear away rock and soil. Wind, rain, rivers, and other natural processes are responsible for most erosion.

extinction: when all the members of a plant or animal species die out

geyser: a natural hot spring that sends fountains of water and steam shooting into the air

glacier: a large body of ice moving slowly across the land

hydroelectric power: electricity produced from the power of rushing water

lava: red-hot melted rock that pours out of volcanoes

magma: lava that is still below the ground

paleontologists: scientists who study fossils to learn about past life on Earth

Paricutín [pah-ree-koo-TEEN]: a volcano in the Mexican state of Michoacán that erupted from 1943 until 1952

petrified wood: wood that has absorbed minerals from the soil and turned rock hard

rain forest: a forest in a region that receives at least 100 inches (254 cm) of rainfall each year

sediment: sand, mud, and minerals that settle to the bottom of a river or other body of water

tectonic plates: giant slabs of rock that form Earth's crust

volcano: an opening in Earth's surface through which melted rock and gases occasionally burst forth

Source Notes

11 Joseph Wallace, *The American Museum of Natural History's Book of Dinosaurs and Other Ancient Creatures* (New York: Simon and Schuster, 1994), 33.

12 Philip Curie, "T-Rex: Back to the Cretaceous," *IMAX*, 1998, http://www.imax.com/t-rex/prodmakingof.html (January 14, 2008).

16 Canadian Heritage Information Network, "Community Memories: The Sinking of the Valencia," *Virtual Museum*, 2008, http://www.virtualmuseum.ca/pm.php?id=story_line &lg=English&fl=0&ex=00000332&sl=8171&pos=1# (January 30, 2008).

27 James Clifford Shirley, "The Redwoods of Coast and Sierra: Discovery of the Redwoods," *nps.gov*, February 2, 2007, http://www.nps.gov/history/history/online-books/shirley/sec2.htm (January 22, 2008).

30 National Park Service, "Muir Woods National Monument," *nps.gov*, January 14, 2008, http://www.nps.gov/muwo (January 22, 2008).

34 Rick Berketa, ed., "Historic Accounts: The Discovery of Niagara Falls," *Thunder Alley*, January 21, 2008, http://www.niagarafrontier.com/accounts.html (December 3, 2007).

38 Joel J. Brattin, *American Journey: Dickens in America*, 2003, http://www.pbs.org/wnet/dickens/life_journeys.html (January 28, 2008).

44 *New York Times*, "The Powell Expedition," July 21, 1869, http://query.nytimes.com/gst/abstract.html?res=9B00E5DC133AEF34BC4951DFB1668382679FDE&scp=58&sq=july+21%2C+1869 (April 16, 2008).

48 Library of Congress, "Maps of Grand Canyon National Park, *American Memory Project: Mapping the Grand Canyon*, January 6, 1999, http://memory.loc.gov/ammem/gmdhtml/nphtml/gchome.html (January 22, 2008).

54 Aubrey L. Haines, "Yellowstone National Park: Its Exploration and Establishment," *nps.gov*, July 4, 2000, http://www.nps.gov/history/history/online_books/haines1/iee1d.htm (October 10, 2007).

61 Yellowstone National Park, "Yellowstone National Park History," *Yellowstone National Park.com*, 2007, http://www.yellowstonenationalpark.com/history.htm 1/23/2008.

65 "The Eruption of Paricutin (1943–1952)," *San Diego State University*, http://www.geology.sdsu.edu/how_volcanoes_work/Paricutin.html (October 10, 2007).

68 Sidney Gruson, "Youngest Volcano Is Scientific 'Lab,'" *New York Times*, February 21, 1952, http://select.nytimes.com/gst/abstract.html?res=F5091FFE395F177B93C3AB1789D85F468585F9&scp=1&sq=youngest+volcano+is+scientific+lab (January 22, 2008).

SELECTED BIBLIOGRAPHY

Barnes-Svarney, Patricia L. *The Oryx Guide to Natural History: The Earth and All Its Inhabitants.* Phoenix: Oryx Press, 1999.

Cleare, John. *Mountains of the World.* San Diego: Thunder Bay Press, 1997.

Collins, Mark, ed. *The Last Rain Forests: A World Conservation Atlas.* New York: Oxford University Press, 1990.

Dolnick, Edward. *Down the Great Unknown: John Wesley Powell's 1890 Journey of Discovery and Tragedy through the Grand Canyon.* New York: HarperCollins, 2001.

Grusin, Richard. *Culture, Technology, and the Creation of America's National Parks.* Cambridge: Cambridge University Press, 2004.

Hanbury-Tenison, Robin. *The Oxford Book of Exploration.* Oxford, UK: Oxford University Press, 1993.

Hancock, Paul, and Brian J. Skinner, eds. *The Oxford Companion to the Earth.* Oxford, UK: Oxford University Press, 2000.

Luhr, James F., ed. *Earth.* London: Dorling Kindersley, 2003.

Man, John, and Chris Schuler. *The Traveler's Atlas.* Hauppage, NY: Barron's Educational Services, 1998.

Moore, Robert J., Jr. *Natural Wonders of the World.* New York: Abbeville Press Publishers, 2000.

Powell, James Lawrence. *Grand Canyon: Solving Earth's Grandest Puzzle.* New York: Pi Press, 2005.

FURTHER READING AND WEBSITES

Books

Braun, Eric. *Canada in Pictures*. Minneapolis: Twenty-First Century Books, 2003. This book explores the geography, history, economy, and cultures of Canada. Readers can learn more about the Canadian province of Alberta, the home of Dinosaur Provincial Park, and about British Columbia, the site of Pacific Rim National Park.

Breining, Greg. *Super Volcano: The Ticking Time Bomb beneath Yellowstone National Park*. Saint Paul: Voyageur Press, 2007. This book describes the Yellowstone Super Volcano and tells what could happen if it were to erupt in the future.

Cone, Patrick. *Grand Canyon*. Minneapolis: Lerner Publications Company, 1994. This book explains the geology of the Grand Canyon, the powerful forces of erosion, how fossils are formed, and the history of the area's earliest peoples.

De Capua, Sarah. *Niagara Falls*. New York: Children's Press, 2002. De Capua takes readers on a tour of this natural wonder and world-famous tourist attraction.

FitzGerald, Dawn. *Julia Butterfly Hill: Saving the Redwoods*. Minneapolis: Lerner Publications Company, 2002. To protest the logging of redwoods, twenty-three-year-old Julia Butterfly Hill lived in a redwood tree for two years. This book tells about her protest and its impact.

Holmes, Thom. *Great Dinosaur Expeditions and Discoveries: Adventures with the Fossil Hunters*. Berkeley Heights, NJ: Enslow Publishers, 2003. People have always been entranced by dinosaurs. Holmes describes some famous expeditions to dig up dinosaur bones, including trips to Alberta and British Columbia.

Kras, Sara Louise. *Redwood*. Logan, IA: Perfection Learning, 2003. This title introduces the world's tallest trees and the other plants and animals that live with them in the forests of the Pacific Northwest coast.

Muir, John. *Nature Writings*. New York: Literary Classics of the United States, 1997. This collection of writings by naturalist John Muir includes descriptions of the areas that became Yellowstone and Yosemite national parks. Muir writes about the grandeur of the natural wilderness and the need to protect it.

Sheldon, David. *Barnum Brown: Dinosaur Hunter*. New York: Walker and Company, 2006. Paleontologist Barnum Brown had a special knack for discovering dinosaur bones. He found *Tyrannosaurus rex* bones in Montana and then went to the Red Deer River area to find more dinosaur bones. This books tells his story.

Skurzynski, Gloria. *Over the Edge: A Mystery in Grand Canyon National Park*. Washington, DC: National Geographic Society, 2002. In this novel for young readers, Jack and Ashley Landon join their veterinarian mother as she tries to solve the mystery of the poisoning of condors in the Grand Canyon. One of the prime suspects is their own foster brother.

Streissguth, Tom. *United States in Pictures*. Minneapolis: Twenty-First Century Books, 2008. The United States is filled with natural wonders, such as Niagara Falls, the Grand

Canyon, and Yellowstone National Park. In this book, Streissguth explores the U.S. landscape, as well as its history, people, and culture.

Woods, Michael, and Mary B. Woods. *Earthquakes*. Minneapolis: Lerner Publications Company, 2007. The Woodses explain how earthquakes occur, how they affect people, and how they have changed the face of Earth.

——. *Volcanoes*. Minneapolis: Lerner Publications Company, 2007. The Woodses explain how volcanoes form, how they have affect people, and how they have altered the face of Earth.

Websites

Niagara Falls: New York State Park
http://www.niagarafallsstatepark.com
This website offers loads of information about the history and geology of Niagara Falls. Visitors will learn about famous people who have visited the falls, how the falls are used to generate electricity, and much more.

Our Amazing Treasures
http://www.nature.ca/discover/treasures/index_e.cfm
This site, sponsored by the Canadian Museum of Nature, has great pictures and information about fossils found in Alberta, including a recently identified horned dinosaur.

Park Vision: Redwood National Park
http://www.shannontech.com/ParkVision/Redwood/Redwood2.html
Redwood National Park is made up of four separate parks along the northern coast of California. At this website, incredible pictures and captions help explain the park's geography, vegetation, and animals.

Royal Tyrrell Museum
http://www.tyrrellmuseum.com
Even if you can't travel to Drumheller, Alberta, to see dinosaur fossils up close, you can view them online. This site tells all about these incredible creatures.

vgsbooks.com
http://www.vgsbooks.com
At the Visual Geography Series® website, you can link to more information about the natural wonders of the United States and Canada.

Yellowstone National Park
http://www.nps.gov/yell/historyculture/index.htm
The U.S. National Park Service created this website about the world's first national park. Visitors can watch videos and podcasts and watch park animals in their natural environment.

INDEX

Africa, 5, 37
Alaska, 20
Alberta, 7, 8, 9, 10, 11, 70
Albertosaurus, 8, 10, 13, 70
American Falls, 34, 35, 37, 40, 41
Angel Falls, 36
Arizona, 43, 70
Asia, 5, 27
Atlantic Ocean, 5, 58
Aztec people, 68

Barkley Sound, 21, 22
Bonaparte, Jérôme, 34
Bonaparte, Napoléon, 34
Bridal Veil Falls, 34, 41
British Columbia, 15
Broken Group Islands, 21, 22, 23
Brown, Barnum, 11, 70

California, 5, 15, 26, 27, 28, 29, 30, 31, 70
Canada, 5, 7, 15, 23, 33, 34, 35, 70; government of, 12, 16, 17, 39; people of, 39
Cárdenas, García López de, 48, 70
Carver, Jonathan, 34
Chandelier Tree, 26
China, 27
Clark, William, 61
Clayoquot Sound, 22
coast redwoods, 5, 31; age of, 27; climate, 26; forests as habitat, 29–30; location, 26, 27; logging, 30–31; natural defenses, 28; size, 25
Colorado, 44
Colorado River, 44–45, 46, 47, 49, 50, 51, 70
Colter, John, 61
Congo River, 37
Congress, 54
Cook, James, 22
Coronado, Francisco Vásquez de, 49
Cortés, Hernán, 68
Crespi, Juan, 27

Currie, Philip, 12

Davis, John C., 54
dawn redwoods, 27
Deer Creek Falls, 51
Dickens, Charles, 38
Dinosaur Provincial Park, 11, 12, 13, 70, 71
dinosaurs, 5, 7, 26; discovery of bones, 8, 10–11; preservation of bones, 9–10; types of, 8–9, 10, 11, 13
Dominion Life Saving Trail, 16
Drumheller, Alberta, 7, 8, 13

El Jorullo Volcano, 68, 70
Europe, 27

Fern Canyon, 29

geysers, 5, 57, 58
Glen Canyon Dam, 49, 50, 70, 71
Grand Canyon, 45, 50, 55, 70, 71; formation of, 44–48; plants and animals, 44; size, 44
Grand Canyon National Park, 49, 50, 70
Grand Canyon of the Yellowstone, 55
Grand River, 43
Gravelot, Jean François "the Great Blondin," 37–38, 70
gray whale, 20
Great Geysir, 58
Great Lakes, 33, 36
Greenland, 5
Gulf of California, 45

Herodotus, 4
Horseshoe Falls, 34, 35, 38, 40, 41
hydroelectric power, 39, 50

Iceland, 58
Idaho, 55
Iroquois, 36, 41

Jackson, William Henry, 54, 70

Johnson, Oscar, 16

Lake Erie, 33, 34, 41
Lake Ontario, 33, 34
Lake Powell, 49, 50, 70
Lewis, Meriwether, 61
Livingstone Falls, 37

Maid of the Mist, 41
Mammoth Hot Springs, 59
maps, 7, 15, 25, 33, 43, 53, 63
Mexico, 5, 20, 46, 63, 70
Mexico City, 63
Michoacán, 63, 69, 70
Minnetaree Indians, 55
Mohave Point, 45
Montana, 55
Monterey Bay, 26
Morning Glory Pool, 59
Mount Everest, 47
Muir, John, 30
Muir Woods National Park, 27

Native Americans, 30, 48, 54, 60–61
New York State, 33, 41
Niagara Escarpment, 34, 40
Niagara Falls, 5, 33, 34, 37, 70; erosion of, 40–41; formation of, 36; islands, 34; for power, 39–40; size, 34. *See also* American Falls; Bridal Veil Falls; Horseshoe Falls
Niagara Reservation State Park, 41
Niagara River, 33, 34, 35, 36, 38, 39, 40
North America, 27; animals of, 5; countries in, 5
North American Plate, 67
Northern Hemisphere, 27
Nuu-chah-nulth people, 22–23

Old Faithful, 5, 54, 57, 58, 61
Ontario, 33, 36, 37, 41
Oregon, 5, 25, 26, 30

Pacific coast, 18, 26, 27, 31
Pacific Ocean, 5, 15, 17, 45, 68
Pacific Plate, 67

Pacific Rim National Park, 21, 22, 23, 70, 71; beaches, 20; climate, 19; formation of, 17; size, 18. *See also* Barkley Sound; Broken Group Islands

Paleo-Indians, 48, 60

Paricutín, 63, 65, 66, 67

Paricutín Volcano: damage by, 65–66, 69, eruptions of, 63–66, 68; formation of, 67, 70; size of, 64

Powell, John Wesley, 44, 49, 70

Prairie Creek Redwoods State Park, 29

prehistoric: animals, 8–9, 48, 68; climate, 9, 26–27, 36, 47–48, 68; people, 68; plants, 26–27, 48, 68

Pulido, Dionisio, 63, 65

Queen Victoria Park, 41

Red Deer River, 7, 10, 11, 70

Redwood National and State Parks, 29, 31, 70, 71

Rocky Mountains, 44, 46, 49

Roosevelt, Theodore, 48

Royal Tyrrell Museum, 8, 12, 13

Russell, Osborne, 61

San Francisco, CA, 16, 27

San Juan Parangaricutiro, 66, 69

sedimentary rock, 9–10, 48

Seven Wonders of the Ancient World, 4

Sierra redwoods, 27

South America, 36

Sternberg, Charles, 11, 70

Tarascan Indians, 68

Taylor, Annie, 38, 70

Trans-Mexican Volcanic Belt, 67–68

trees, 19, 28, 29

Tyrrell, Joseph B., 7, 8, 10, 70

United Nations Educational, Scientific, and Cultural Organization (UNESCO), 13, 31, 51, 61

United States, 5, 26, 33, 34, 46, 54; cities of, 36, 37; government of, 39, 49, 54, 61, 70; people of, 39

Utah, 49

Valencia, 16, 70

Vancouver, George, 17, 70

Vancouver Island, 5, 20, 21, 22, 70; shipwrecks, 15–17; size, 15

Venezuela, 36

volcanoes, 5, 64–65, 66–67

Washington, D.C., 54

West Coast Trail, 17, 71

West Thumb Geyser Basin, 58

World Heritage Site, 13, 31, 51, 61, 70, 71

Wyoming, 53, 55

Yellowstone Falls, 55

Yellowstone Lake, 55, 56

Yellowstone National Park, 5, 54, 56, 61, 70, 71; location of, 55; plants and animals, 59–60; size of, 55

Yellowstone River, 55, 56

Yellowstone River valley, 5, 53, 54, 70

Yellowstone Super Volcano, 56

ABOUT THE AUTHORS

Michael Woods is a science and medical journalist in Washington, D.C. He has won many national writing awards. Mary B. Woods is a school librarian. Their past books include the eight-volume Ancient Technology series, the fifteen-volume Disasters Up Close series, and the seven-volume Ancient Wonders of the World books. The Woodses have four children. When not writing, reading, or enjoying their grandchildren, the Woodses travel to gather material for future books.

PHOTO ACKNOWLEDGMENTS

The images in this book are used with the permission of: © Macduff Everton/Riser/Getty Images, p. 5; © Yves Marcoux/First Light/Getty Images, p. 6; © Laura Westlund/Independent Picture Service, pp. 7, 15, 25, 33, 43, 53, 63; Photo courtesy of the Royal Tyrrell Museum, Drumheller, Alberta , p. 8; © Steve Estvanik/Dreamstime.com, pp. 10 (top), 13; © Verena Matthew/Dreamstime.com, p. 10 (bottom); © Louie Psihoyos/Science Faction/Getty Images, pp. 11, 12, 72 (center right); © Chris Cheadle/All Canada Photos/Getty Images, pp. 14, 18, 21 bottom, 22, 72 (bottom right); University of Washington Libraries, Special Collections, TRA765, p. 16; © Josh McCulloch/All Canada Photos/Getty Images, p. 17; © Henry Georgi/Aurora/Getty Images, p. 19 (left); © Chris Howes/Wild Places Photography/Alamy, p. 19 (right); © Jeremy Koreski/All Canada Photos/Getty Images, p. 20 (top); © Flip Nicklin/Minden Pictures, p. 20 (bottom); © Tim Stach/drr.net, p. 21 (top); © British Museum/Art Resource, NY, p. 23 (top); © Dirk Enters/imagebroker/Alamy, p. 23 (bottom); © Ted Spiegel/National Geographic/Getty Images, p. 24; © Steven Vidler/Eurasia Press/CORBIS, p. 26 (top); © Philippe Bourseiller/The Image Bank/Getty Images, p. 26 (bottom); © iStockphoto.com/Rafael Ramirez Lee, pp. 27, 72 (top right); © Marc Moritsch/National Geographic/Getty Images, p. 28 (top); © iStockphoto.com/Del Kienholz, p. 28 (bottom); © Carr Clifton/Minden Pictures/Getty Images, p. 29 (top); © Fabian Gonzales Editorial/Alamy, p. 29 (bottom); Library of Congress (LC-DIG-npcc-20069), p. 30; © VCL/Taxi/Getty Images, p. 32; © Laura Ciapponi/Photonica/Getty Images, p. 35 (top); © Darwin Wiggett/First Light/Getty Images, p. 35 (bottom left); © Per Breiehagen/The Image Bank/Getty Images, p. 35 (bottom right); © Images Etc Ltd/Photographer's Choice/Getty Images, p. 36; Niagara Falls Heritage Foundation Collection/Niagara Falls Public Library, pp. 37, 38 (both); AP Photo/David Duprey, p. 39; © Skip Brown/National Geographic/Getty Images, p. 40; © age fotostock/SuperStock, p. 41; © Richard Price/Photographer's Choice/Getty Images, p. 42; Utah State Historical Society, used by permission, all rights reserved, p. 44; © Tim Fitzharris/Minden Pictures/Getty Images, p. 45; © Norbert Wu/Minden Pictures/Getty Images, p. 46; Mark Lellouch/National Park Service, pp. 47, 49, 51 (bottom), 72 (top center); © Photodisc/Getty Images, p. 50; National Park Service, p. 51 (top); © Alexander Stewart/Riser/Getty Images, p. 52; © Michael Melford/Riser/Getty Images, p. 55; William Henry Jackson Collection/Scotts Bluff National Monument, p. 54; © Norbert Rosing/National Geographic/Getty Images, p. 56; © Panoramic Images/Getty Images, p. 57; Frank Balthis/National Park Service, p. 58; © Andy Holligan/Dorling Kindersley/Getty Images, p. 59 (top); © Jeff Foot/Discovery Channel Images/Getty Images, p. 59 (bottom); © David Schultz/Stone/Getty Images, p. 60 (top); Jim Peaco/National Park Service, p. 60 (bottom); U.S. Geological Survey, pp. 62, 67, 72 (top left); U.S. Geological Survey/E. Ordonez, pp. 64 (top), 65; U.S. Geological Survey/R. Morrow, p. 64 (bottom); © SuperStock, p. 66; © Kerry Graham/Spectrumphotofile, p. 69; © iStockphoto.com/Li Kim Goh, p. 72 (bottom left); © Gustav Verderber/Visuals Unlimited/Getty Images, p. 72 (bottom center);

Front cover: © iStockphoto.com/Rafael Ramirez Lee (top left); © Louie Psihoyos/Science Faction/Getty Images (top center); © iStockphoto.com/Li Kim Goh (top right); Mark Lellouch/National Park Service (center); U.S. Geological Survey (bottom left); © Gustav Verderber/Visuals Unlimited/Getty Images (bottom center); © Chris Cheadle/All Canada Photos/Getty Images (bottom right).